D1368511

Chinien
2/15

AMAZING
FOOTBALL
RECORDS

BY THOM STORDEN

Reading Consultant:
Barbara J. Fox
Professor Emerita
North Carolina State University

CAPSTONE PRESS
a capstone imprint

Blazers Books are published by Capstone Press,
1710 Roe Crest Drive, North Mankato, Minnesota 56003
www.capstonepub.com

Library of Congress Cataloging-in-Publication Data
Storden, Thom.
  Amazing football records / by Thom Storden.
pages cm.—(Blazers books. Epic sports records.)
Includes bibliographical references and index.
Summary: "Provides information on the most stunning records in the sport of
professional football"—Provided by publisher.
ISBN 978-1-4914-0743-1 (library binding)
ISBN 978-1-4914-0748-6 (ebook pdf)
1. Football--Records—Juvenile literature. I. Title.
GV955.S84 2015
 796.332—dc23
                              2014008656

Editorial Credits
Nate LeBoutillier, editor; Kyle Grenz, designer; Eric Gohl, media researcher;
Kathy McColley, production specialist

Photo Credits
AP Photo: Ed Zurga, 9, Greg Trott, cover (top), Pro Football Hall of Fame, 28;
Dreamstime: Jerry Coli, 10, 19, 23; Getty Images: Focus on Sport, 25, 26, Rick
Stewart, 12; Newscom: Ai Wire Photo Service/Edward Larson, 5, Icon SMI, 15,
MCT/Carlos Gonzalez, cover (bottom), 7, Sports Chrome/Bob Tringali, 20, ZUMA
Press, 17; Shutterstock: David Lee, 2–3, 30–31, 32, imaging, 1

Design Elements: Shuttestock

Records in this book are current through the 2013 season.

Printed in the United States of America in Stevens Point, Wisconsin.
032014   008092WZF14

TABLE OF CONTENTS

HOW DO WE MEASURE AMAZING?

Football is a very **competitive** sport. How do we separate the best from the rest? How do we give credit to incredible performances? How do we make glorious moments into golden memories? Keeping records is one way to do it.

competitive—trying to be the best

Joe Montana won four Super Bowls. Montana and Terry Bradshaw are the only quarterbacks to do so.

JOE MONTANA

MOST RUSHING YARDS IN ONE GAME
296

On November 4, 2007, Adrian Peterson rambled. He galloped. He bulldozed. He smashed. And when the game was over, the **tenacious** running back had set a remarkable record. Peterson had rushed for 296 yards—the most ever—as his Minnesota Vikings beat the San Diego Chargers.

OTHER SINGLE-GAME PLAYER RECORDS

Most Yards Receiving

336 Flipper **Anderson**
Los Angeles Rams, November 26, 1989

Most Yards Passing

554 Norm **Van Brocklin**
Los Angeles Rams, September 28, 1951

EPIC//FACT

Adrian Peterson set the single-game rushing record in his rookie season. It was just his eighth game as a pro.

ADRIAN PETERSON

tenacious–never giving up
rookie–a first-year player

7

MOST PASSING TOUCHDOWNS IN A SEASON 55

In the Denver Broncos' first game of 2013, quarterback Peyton Manning threw seven touchdowns. He went on to break the record for passing touchdowns in a season by throwing a total of 55. Manning also broke the record for passing yards in a season with 5,477.

OTHER OFFENSIVE PLAYER RECORDS

Most Touchdowns Scored

31	LaDainian **Tomlinson** San Diego Chargers, 2006

Most Touchdowns Caught

23	Randy **Moss** New England Patriots, 2007

PEYTON MANNING

EPIC//FACT

Peyton Manning sat out the entire 2011 season with a neck injury. At that time, some fans thought he might never play again.

EPIC//FACT

Emmitt Smith rushed for over 1,000 yards in 11 straight seasons.

EMMITT SMITH

MOST RUSHING YARDS IN A CAREER

18,355

For 15 years running back Emmitt Smith took **handoffs** in the NFL. He played for the Dallas Cowboys and the Arizona Cardinals. When he retired in 2004, he had rushed for 18,355 yards. That equals roughly 10.4 miles (16.7 kilometers).

OTHER INDIVIDUAL CAREER RECORDS

Most Rushing Touchdowns

164 Emmitt **Smith**, Dallas Cowboys, Arizona Cardinals, 1990–2004

Most Receiving Touchdowns

197 Jerry **Rice**, San Francisco 49ers, Oakland Raiders, Seattle Seahawks, 1985–2004

handoff—when the quarterback gives the ball to a rusher

FRANK REICH

EPIC//FACT

The Bills' epic comeback was led by back-up quarterback Frank Reich. But Reich had done it before. He once led a 31-point comeback in a college game.

BIGGEST COMEBACK OF ALL TIME 32 POINTS

In a 1993 playoff game, the Buffalo Bills were getting stomped. By the third quarter, the Houston Oilers were ahead 35–3. But then the Bills **rallied** to tie the score at 38. The Bills won in overtime, completing the biggest comeback ever.

OTHER SINGLE-GAME TEAM RECORDS

Most Points

73 Chicago **Bears** versus Washington Redskins, December 8, 1940

Most Yards Gained

735 Los Angeles **Rams** versus New York Yanks, September 28, 1951

rally–to come back from losing

13

BEST RECORD IN A SEASON 17-0

Never before had a pro football team finished a season **undefeated** and untied. The 1972 Miami Dolphins changed that by winning all 17 of their games, including the Super Bowl. The Dolphins featured great team play and the coaching of Don Shula.

OTHER SINGLE-SEASON TEAM RECORDS

Worst Record
0-16 Detroit **Lions**, 2008

Most Points
589 New England **Patriots**, 2007

undefeated–never beaten

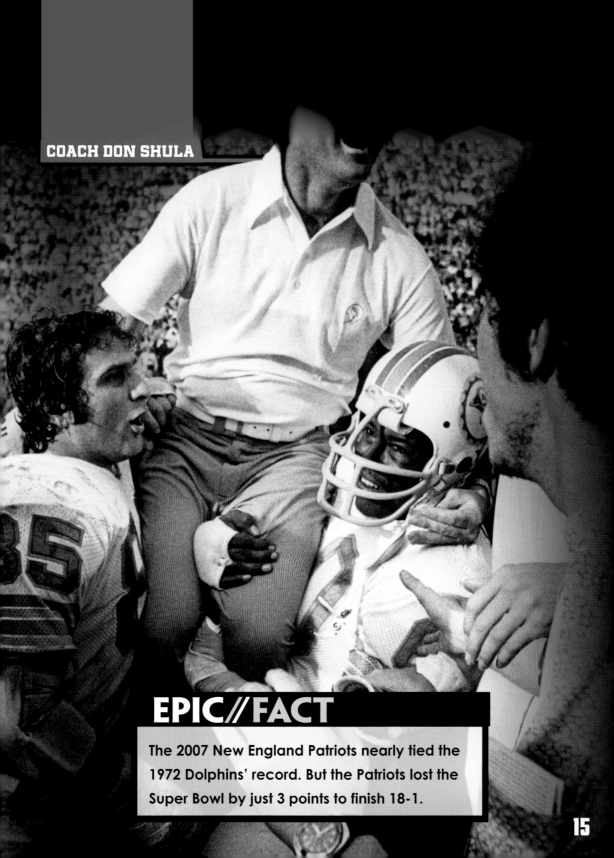

COACH DON SHULA

EPIC//FACT

The 2007 New England Patriots nearly tied the 1972 Dolphins' record. But the Patriots lost the Super Bowl by just 3 points to finish 18-1.

MOST SUPER BOWL WINS 6

The Pittsburgh Steelers defeated the Arizona Cardinals 27–23 to win Super Bowl XLIII. The victory gave Pittsburgh six Super Bowl titles—the most of all time. Other seasons the Steelers won the Super Bowl include 1974, 1975, 1978, 1979, and 2005.

OTHER TEAM RECORDS

Most Consecutive Winning Seasons

20 Dallas **Cowboys**, 1966–1985

Most Consecutive Games Won

22 New England **Patriots**, 2003–2004

EPIC//FACT

The Dallas Cowboys and San Francisco 49ers have each won five Super Bowls.

SUPER BOWL-WINNING STEELERS RECEIVER SANTONIO HOLMES

MOST POSTSEASON TOUCHDOWNS

22

Jerry Rice was a blur on the turf. The speedy wide receiver also had hands as sticky as maple syrup. So maybe it's no surprise that he holds many records. He was at his best in the **postseason**, where he scored 22 touchdowns. Rice also helped the San Francisco 49ers win three Super Bowls.

OTHER POSTSEASON INDIVIDUAL PLAYER RECORDS

Career Receptions

151 Jerry **Rice**, San Francisco 49ers, Oakland Raiders

Career Rushing Touchdowns

19 Emmitt **Smith**, Dallas Cowboys

postseason—the games after the regular season; playoff games

JERRY RICE

EPIC//FACT

Jerry Rice caught a record eight touchdowns in the four Super Bowls he played in during his 20-year career.

KURT WARNER

EPIC//FACT

Kurt Warner has the top three passing yardage games in Super Bowl history.

MOST YARDS PASSING IN A SUPER BOWL
414

Kurt Warner did not make the NFL right after college. Instead he worked at a grocery store. He finally made it at age 27 with the St. Louis Rams. In 1999 Warner led the Rams to the Super Bowl title and threw for a record 414 yards.

OTHER SUPER BOWL RECORDS

Most Yards Rushing
204 — Timmy **Smith**
Washington Redskins, Super Bowl XXII

Most Yards Receiving
215 — Jerry **Rice**
San Francisco 49ers, Super Bowl XXIII

ONLY TEAM to WIN BACK-TO-BACK SUPER BOWLS TWICE

The Pittsburgh Steelers were the **dominant** team of the 1970s. They won back-to-back Super Bowls in 1975–76 and 1978–79. The offense was led by quarterback Terry Bradshaw, running back Franco Harris, and wide receiver Lynn Swann. The defense was mean and tough.

OTHER SUPER BOWL TEAM RECORDS

Most Consecutive Super Bowl Appearances

4 Buffalo **Bills**, 1990–1993

Most Overall Super Bowl Appearances

8 Dallas **Cowboys** and Pittsburgh **Steelers**

dominant–most powerful

TERRY BRADSHAW

EPIC//FACT

Terry Bradshaw won back-to-back Super Bowl MVP honors in the 1978 and 1979 seasons.

AGE OF THE OLDEST PLAYER OF ALL TIME 48

George Blanda broke into pro football as a quarterback with the Chicago Bears. In 1949 he was just a 22-year-old quarterback. Twenty-six years later Blanda was still playing. He played for the Bears, Baltimore Colts, Houston Oilers, and Oakland Raiders.

OTHER UNBELIEVABLE RECORDS

Most Seasons with One Team

21 Jason **Hanson**, kicker, Detroit Lions, 1992–2012

Most Games Played, All Time

382 Morten **Andersen**, kicker, five teams, 1982–2007

GEORGE BLANDA

EPIC//FACT

George Blanda played both quarterback and kicker in his pro career. In 1961 he led the league with 36 touchdown passes.

EPIC//FACT

Quarterback Brett Favre fumbled 166 times in his career, more than any other player.

MOST FUMBLES IN A GAME BY A SINGLE PLAYER 7

Was it raining? Snowing? Sleeting? It was not. But you might have thought so the way quarterback Len Dawson handled the football on November 15, 1964. That day Dawson fumbled the ball seven times and threw two interceptions. Needless to say, his team lost.

OTHER EMBARRASSING RECORDS

Most Interceptions Thrown in One Season

42 George **Blanda**, Houston Oilers, 1962

Most Interceptions Thrown in One Game

8 Jim **Hardy**, Chicago Cardinals versus Philadelphia Eagles, September 24, 1950

ERNIE NEVERS

EPIC//FACT

Ernie Nevers played three seasons of
pro baseball for the St. Louis Browns.
As a pitcher he gave up two home
runs to the great Babe Ruth in 1927.

MOST POINTS SCORED IN ONE GAME BY A SINGLE PLAYER 40

One of pro football's oldest records is also one of the most amazing. On November 28, 1929, Ernie Nevers set it when he scored 40 points in a single game. The Chicago Cardinals beat the Chicago Bears in the game. Nevers scored 6 touchdowns and kicked 4 **PATs**.

OTHER AMAZING EFFORT RECORDS

Consecutive Starts, Including Playoffs

321 Brett **Favre**, September 27, 1992, to December 5, 2010

Most Coaching Wins

347 Don **Shula**, 1963–1995

PAT–stands for Point After Touchdown

GLOSSARY

competitive (kum-PET-i-tiv)—trying to be the best

dominant (DOM-uh-nuhnt)—most powerful

handoff (HAND-off)—when the quarterback gives the ball to a rusher

PAT—stands for Point After Touchdown

postseason (POST-see-sun)—the games after the regular season; playoff games

rally (RAL-ee)—to come back from losing

rookie (RUK-ee)—a first-year player

tenacious (ten-AY-shus)—never giving up

undefeated (un-dee-FEE-ted)—never beaten

READ MORE

Levit, Joseph, Tim Gramling, Steven Bennett, and Zachary Cohen. *Sports Illustrated Kids STATS!* New York: Time Home Entertainment, Inc. 2013.

Frederick, Shane. *The Best of Everything Football Book.* North Mankato, Minn.: Capstone Press, 2011.

INTERNET SITES

FactHound offers a safe, fun way to find Internet sites related to this book. All of the sites on FactHound have been researched by our staff.

Here's all you do:

Visit *www.facthound.com*

Type in this code: 9781491407431

Super-cool stuff! Check out projects, games and lots more at
www.capstonekids.com

INDEX